Soaring To New Heights

on the

Wings of Eagles

*A Treasury of Affirmations and
Quotations for Personal Achievement*

Carleen Franklin

Sarah LaPlant

Soaring To New Heights On The Wings of Eagles

A Treasury of Affirmations and Quotations
for Personal Achievement

Carleen Franklin and Sarah LaPlant

Published by Excelerators
1631 S.E. 24th Boulevard
Okeechobee, Florida 34974
(813) 467-5350 or (800) 232-5350
Fax: (813) 467-5359

Cover design by Jim Pollard

Kaludas ©
by Robin Franklin Nigh

Revised Edition
Copyright © 1995
ISBN: 0-964087-1-9

Printed in the United States of America

Introduction

By the age of three, we know most of the conversational words we'll use for the rest of our lives. All of our lives we subconsciously invoke the feelings we felt when we first learned and used a particular word. Adults hear a word which creates the pictures associated with that word. We then feel the feelings associated with it.

The use of repetition is a natural trait of the very young as they explore the excitement of learning. Repetition can be used at any age to learn, relearn or change habits and/or behavior. *Soaring to New Heights* shares ideas for choosing and making changes and goes a step further, sharing ideas on how to compose and use affirmations. Positive repetition in the first person (I, me, mine) is considered a direct route to our subconscious mind. The mind accepts the statement as true when it is written, read or repeated in the first person.

Using this technique is how we made the transition from pitiful to powerful. Try it, you have everything to gain. . . and it's really great soaring with the Eagles.

Dedication

The ideas and words in this book are dedicated to the people with BIG hearts who helped me, and loved me enough to share their ideas - most did not even know me. Their humanity drove them to share, and I thank them.

It is also dedicated to the people who allow me into their lives to pass this information on.

And also to Sarah, my "forever friend," who noticed my isolation and offered her hand and heart in a selfless friendship. Her kind acts of friendship are having a ripple effect that will last for generations.

Carleen

The affirmations, quotations and thoughts in this book are dedicated to the many individuals who recognized the potential within me. They encouraged me to set goals and reach for them, accomplishing much more than I ever dreamed possible.

A special thanks to my friend, Carleen, whose knowledge and courage I greatly admire, whose love was unconditional, and whose friendship is forever.

Sarah

TABLE OF CONTENTS

Introduction. iii

Adventure 1

Words 15

Qualities 25

Success 33

Power 47

Growth 59

Friends 71

Love 81

Faith 89

Affirmation techniques . . 99

Adventure

"People must learn to gather adventures and experiences rather than things and possessions.

Possessions will burden you; adventures become memories which will enrich your soul and last forever."

Alfred A. Montapert

"I remember that I am endowed with the same awesome power as the most magnificent eagle.

I spread my wings and soar into my life's ADVENTURE."

Carleen and Sarah

My Life Is An Ongoing
ADVENTURE

Attitude

Destination / Goals

Visualization / View

Enthusiasm

New Ideas

Thoughts/ Talk

Using my power

Responsibility

Expectations

"It takes time, patience, and practice
to develop the power within me for
the Adventure of living
my life more abundantly."
        Carleen and Sarah

Attitude

simply means the way I feel about
something - my opinion.

*"My attitude at the beginning of a task
more than anything else will
determine its outcome."*
                             Earl Nightingale

I control my attitude with words.

Attitudes are not inherited. I change
my attitude by CHOOSING to.

*"The greatest revelations of our generation
is the discovery that human beings,
by changing the inner attitudes
of their minds can change the outer
aspects of their lives."*
                             William James

My Attitude Influences My Success In Everything I Do !

I present an attitude of success !
My attitude affects all around me !

I take the responsibility to keep my own attitude positive in spite of negatives around me.

Since attitudes are formed by imagination, response to others, and/or environment, then imagination can change my attitudes.

Words alone applied to imagination can change attitudes, thus changing behavior.

Destination - Goals

Goals Are Vital To My Happiness and Success

Destination: The purpose for which someone is destined; the place toward which one is going - a goal.

Goal: An object or end that one strives to attain.

I have a purpose ! I have a destiny !

I choose what I want in life and write it down. I occasionally re-write my goals as I achieve some.

I look at my goals every day.

I am worthy of all goals I thoughtfully set.

My goals help others by setting the example of accomplishment.

My goals are for the good of many.

I expect to reach my goals.

I intend to reach my goals !

Visualization - Views

Visualizing Helps Me Achieve My Goals !

View/Visualize: Range of vision, manner of regarding something; to see, behold a mental image.

I choose my views for myself.

I look *forward* with great anticipation.

I have high self esteem - I view myself worthy of great accomplishments.

My self image is beautiful; powerful.

I forgive myself for all errors.

I remember my successes.

I visualize a wonderful present and an exciting, magnificent future.

"Looking forward is being open to the advantages and opportunities waiting for me when I surrender to my destiny."

Carleen and Sarah

Enthusiasm

Enthusiasm: Evidence of my belief!
Intense or eager interest; zeal.

I am enthusiastic !

I enjoy sharing my enthusiasm.

I greet people with enthusiasm.

I share sincere compliments when
I meet others.

I sincerely SEE people as wonderful.

To renew my enthusiasm, I read
affirmations and tell myself
"Life is an Adventure!"

I am enthusiastic about life !

New Ideas

New Ideas Are Exciting !

NEW: Discovered, unfamiliar, fresh, more, additional.
IDEAS: Thought, mental image, opinion or belief.

I love hearing and trying new ideas !

"Progress is impossible if I am only willing to do things the way they have always been done."
         Albert Einstein

I eagerly try new ideas.

I trust my subconscious to inspire me and lead me to new ideas.

I enjoy taking new paths in my mind and new routes in my daily travels.

"It is obvious we cannot use the same thinking to solve the problem that we have been using to cause it."
         Albert Einstein

THOUGHTS and SELF TALK
Thoughts Have Awesome Power !

"The thoughts that come unsought, and, as it were, drop into the mind, are commonly the most valuable of any we have."
John Locke

My life is affected by the way I talk to myself.
I am talking to myself 94% of the time in thoughts - words only I can hear.

I think in words,
   they create the thoughts,
      then I see the pictures created.
         The pictures create the feelings.

All this thousands of times faster than
the greatest computer ever invented.

*"As long as one keeps searching,
the answers come."*
Joan Baez

USE THE POWER

**I was born with the
power of the universe !**

I enjoy renewing my personal power.

My subconscious mind is constant energy
and it never sleeps.   My mind is always
working to reach the goals I have set.

I surrender to my subconscious;
my intuition guides me.

When I set a goal, I plug into my universal
power which helps me achieve the goal.

I am my own expert - I am not affected
by negatives around me.

I use my personal power to help
myself and others grow.

*"By keeping my mind open, I'm sure
to learn something new everyday."*
                             Jodie Carol

RESPONSIBILITY

Responsible: Answerable or accountable, as for something within one's power, control, or management.

I willingly accept responsibility !

The responsibility is mine . . . completely . . . for my life, my decisions, my priorities, and my goals.

Accepting full responsibility for my actions and decisions gives me the power and freedom to choose to be what I want to be and to do what I want to do with my life.

Challenges may cause me to reevaluate my priorities occasionally and sometimes set new goals altogether.

I accept the responsibility to make today special.

I Am Responsible For My Own Behavior !

What happens around me is largely outside my control . . .

How I choose to react to what happens is within my control !

When I become upset by what another person says or does, I remember they have the right to be themselves.

I avoid criticizing others and build them up with my positive reactions.

I may be responsible **to** other people, but I am not responsible **for** their actions.

I AM responsible for my own thoughts and actions.

EXPECTATIONS

Expectations are self fulfilling prophecies !

I expect the best from myself.

I treat others with respect and expect
the best from each person I meet.

Everyone is competent in some way,
and I address the competent part.

I accept that I have the power and
freedom of an Eagle
and I expect to
soar with success.

**I believe God has created my spirits
with wings to fly in the spacious
firmament of love and freedom !**

Words

"Do not become anxious how you are to speak . . . for what you are to say will be given to you in that hour."

Matthew 10:19

"Words are the magic keys that can unlock and open doors previously closed to us!"

Carleen and Sarah

I Believe My Thoughts Really Affect My Life.

"If I think I can, or if I think I can't, either way I'm right."
                                    Henry Ford

Words are the tools with which to implement changes I choose to make !

I choose what I think and say to myself and others very carefully.

I always keep my thoughts positive and upbeat - I know my subconscious is listening and I feed it wonderful constructive words.

By controlling my conscious thoughts, I control my emotions.

I take excellent, loving care of my thoughts and self talk.

"For as he thinketh in his heart, so is he."
                                    Proverbs 23:7

Words That Are Meaningful To Me.

Courtesy

I enjoy being polite.

Honesty

I am proud to say I am
honest in thoughts and deeds.

Appearance

I feel good about my appearance.
If I cannot change some things about
me, I ignore them.

Service

I am on this earth to serve God.
Taking care of myself is a trust to him;
caring for others a service.

*Kind words lift me up -
they are more precious than
gems or beautiful flowers.*

Words Are The Access Codes To Make The Changes I Choose To Make In My Life !

All the resources needed to make
me successful are within me.

My mind works like a computer and
I am the operator with the power to change.

I can become the person I want to be
and do the things I choose by using
words to re-program my subconscious.

By changing negative thoughts to
positive, happy thoughts, I am able
to control my feelings.

When I hear negative words, I
subconsciously ignore them, and I
repeat positive thoughts to myself.

I AM IN CONTROL OF MY OWN MIND !

"PLEASE"
Is A Wonderful Word !

I have learned how to use PLEASE to make all my relationships better.

"Please" tell me what you are thinking.

"Please" tell me why you feel that way.

"Please" tell me how I can help.

Probe - ask others about their thoughts and feelings.

Listen - attentively to answers and tone of voice.

Empathize - with genuine understanding.

Anticipate - the best response - we get what we expect.

Sincerely - show I care about their feelings.

Evaluate and **accept** others' responses.

I Realize Anger Is Caused By Hurt !

I am slow to anger.

I realize "hurt" can be controlled.

I control my own feelings.

When I feel angry, I am reasonable and carefully consider the reason.

I handle anger well.

When I am disappointed in another, I am still responsible for only my own feelings.

I avoid "you" accusations.

I use "I" messages when explaining my feelings.

"I" don't understand - please explain.

"The Lord is merciful and gracious, slow to anger and plenteous in mercy."
Psalms 103:8

REASON is the ability to think,
draw conclusions, good sense,
to think logically.

REASONABLE is just, fair, sensible,
wise, not excessive.

UNREASONABLE is excessive,
immoderate, and irrational.

I am reasonable in my expectations
of myself and others.

I trust myself to have an answer.

I react to changes and challenges by
looking for a better way.

When others are unreasonable in their
expectations of me, I consult
my inner power to cope.

I resist pressure from outside with
confidence in my own inner voice.

I rely on my inner power.

Anything Worth Doing Is Worth Doing Right.

*"What we have to learn to do,
we learn by doing."*
                            Aristotle

I trust in the ultimate good planned
for me, therefore I always
do my best in all ways.

When I have a responsibility to do
something, I study the situation,
rehearse my part, choose
my words and actions carefully,
picture the end results, and
expect the best !

I tape record ideas and replay them
for positive preparation.

***"To utter pleasant words without
practicing them is like a fine flower
without fragrance."***
                            Buddha

I "Should" Have Read This Book A Long Time Ago !

I shall never "should" on myself
or anyone else again.

I shall remember to avoid using
"I should," you "should," or
anyone else "should."

I realize nothing can be changed
that is past, nor can I ever
change anyone else !

I can only change the present -
My Own:
> Thoughts,
> Attitudes,
> Actions.

**I learn from putting
my thoughts in writing.**

Qualities

*"The sculpture is already in the rock
before the chisel is ever raised.
All the qualities I choose to develop
are already in me. I continue
to carve my way to greatness."*

Carleen and Sarah

*"Greatness after all, in spite
of its name,
appears to be not so much
a certain size as a
certain quality in human lives."*

Phillips Brooks

I Have Identified The Key Qualities To Develop For Personal Growth.

QUALITY: *A characteristic, attribute, trait, endowment, individuality, style, personality or temperament.*

Qualities are LEARNED
and
can be CHANGED !

The Key Qualities I can develop are:

Friendliness
Respect
Enthusiasm
Sincerity
Helpfulness

I have a F R E S H approach to personal growth and self management.

FRIENDLINESS:

Showing people that I like and respect them; showing kindness in all situations; being amiable and congenial.

I eagerly anticipate meeting new people - new friends.

I maintain my pleasant expression even when confronted with an unpleasant situation.

I carefully listen to the other person without interrupting and I attempt to understand.

I am kind and patient even when I do not understand the situation.

I am in control of myself, and I keep an open mind.

My attitude reflects my friendliness.

RESPECT:

*Courtesy, consideration, regard,
active listening, punctuality.*

I respect the earth, the animals, and
the Universal Power guiding me.

I respect myself, my uniqueness,
my goals, and my life's plan.

I respect others' rights to be themselves.

I am always polite and courteous to
every person I encounter.

I listen with respect even when opinions
are different from mine.

I Am Always On Time !

I understand being on time for
appointments - even with friends
and family - shows love and respect.

**Respect means practicing the
Golden Rule !**

ENTHUSIASM:

Animation, eagerness, eloquence, obvious willingness.

Enthusiasm is evidence of my belief.

I carefully put "extra" emotional intensity in my voice.

I practice acting enthusiastically.

I always avoid fault finding - in myself as well as others - this helps me maintain my enthusiasm.

When I need to renew my enthusiasm, I think of my goals and I get excited.

I enjoy being around enthusiastic people, and I seek them out.

Believing I have a purpose in life keeps me enthusiastic.

SINCERITY:

Believing in the truth of what I am saying; honesty, frankness, openness, reliability.

I am always truthful and honest. If the truth would hurt someone, I am silent and do not speak.

I have the self confidence and personal power to be open in my feelings.

Others enjoy my frankness, yet I am very careful of their feelings.

I am dependable and reliable.

I am proud that I always keep my word.

Being sincere increases my self esteem.

I feel good about me !

HELPFULNESS:

Showing willingness to go out of my way to assist others and showing enjoyment of doing so, assistance, propriety, convenience, usefulness, adaptability.

I enjoy sharing and helping others.

When I cannot accommodate a request, I am still polite and tactful.

I willingly change my plans to accommodate others when it is appropriate.

I am a caring person and offer assistance to those less fortunate.

I do for others without expecting anything in return.

I am in this world to make a difference.

I help others at every opportunity.

Success

*"There is only one success -
to be able to spend your life
in your own way."*

Christopher Morley

*"I will instruct and guide you in the
best path for you. I will advise
you and watch your progress."*

Psalm 32:8

I Want To Grow !

"It is never too late to be what I might have been."
                                George Eliot

I can start today . . .
    To do what I've missed,
      To love myself,
        To love others,
          To learn more,
            To give more.

Grandma Moses painted over 1,000 paintings after she was 69 years old. She painted 25% of her greatest paintings after she was 100.

"I locked the door on yesterday, and threw the key away.

Tomorrow has no fears for me, since I have found today!"
                                Author Unknown

I Tell Myself I CAN Make My Own Choices !

I CAN choose my own goals -
my own path.

I CAN share myself with others -
I have a lot to give; to share.

I CAN handle anything.

I CAN be happy!

I CHOOSE happiness.

I CHOOSE sharing.

I CHOOSE with confidence!

I CHOOSE success !

*"There are only two lasting bequests
we can hope to give our children.
One of these is roots,
the other wings."*
                    Hodding Carter

I CAN Make A Difference !

"To understand the heart and mind of a person, look not at what they have already achieved, but at what they aspire to do."
       Kahlil Gibran

I aspire to make a difference.

I want to serve my fellow man
and fulfill my destiny.

I choose to live life to the fullest.

My dreams are achievable.

I am powerful and I enjoy helping
others reach their potential.

As I guide others, I am patient
with their progress.

"If you are content with the best you have done, you will never do the best you can do."
       Martin Vanbee

I shall always strive to be better !

I WANT to make a difference !

I *INTEND* to make a difference !

"**Want**" is a moment to moment thing,

"**Intention**" is a determination to accomplish.

INTENTION is:

- To have in mind a plan or aim,
- Being responsible,
- Making a commitment,
- Follow through,
- Dependability,
- Determination to do a specific act in a specified manner.

I INTEND to live up to my pre-destined, magnificent potential.

True Happiness Comes From Within

*"Happiness is a perfume you cannot
pour on others without getting
a few drops on yourself."*
    Author Unknown

Happiness comes not from exterior
situations, but from the peace within me.

Joy is never in things, it is in ME.

I do not wait for others to
"make me happy."

My happiness is internal and by
reminding myself I am a valuable
Child of God, I can take action to
help myself grow.

**Personal growth brings me
personal happiness.**

*"Action may not always bring happiness;
but there is no happiness without action."*
    Disraeli

Proper Preparation Provide Positive Performance !

When I have a "job" to do, I plan ahead, and I am always prepared.

I always get jobs done on time.

I am proud of my follow through!

I am a very organized person.

I have the power and ability to accomplish whatever I set my mind to.

I have pride in my performance and a positive expectancy of the future.

"You are what you set out to be. The things you read and the thoughts you think are the things you become tomorrow."
Forbes

Successful People Don't Like To Do The Same Things Unsuccessful People Don't Like To Do -

We Just DO Them ANYWAY.

When I feel I could "drop out", I
remind myself of the alternative.

I am proud of myself as I keep my
promises to myself and to others.

I am dedicated to personal growth
and personal responsibility
to myself and my ideals.

Words encourage me to move
forward to success.

I Am Successful !

I Handle Each Day As It Comes !

*"One can never consent to creep
when one feels an impulse to soar."*
Plus: The Magazine of Positive Thinking

I greet each day with enthusiasm.

I avoid worrying about anything
in advance.

Every day I am more comfortable
with my patience.

I plan ahead and enjoy today.

Today is the best day of my life
and I rejoice in it !

*"The million little things that drop into
our hands, the small opportunities each day
brings; He leaves us free to use or abuse
and goes unchanging along His silent way."*
Helen Keller

I Quietly Do Helping And Worthwhile Things For My Friends.

I am warm and friendly toward all.

I treat everyone with consideration and respect.

I do a kindness for someone everyday.

When I'm not "sure" of what I should be doing, I do "something."

I am constantly alert for ways to help others.

I have an ever growing, supportive group of friends. We help each other in great and small ways.

"Small deeds done are better than great deeds planned."
Peter Marshall

CHANGE Is Essential To Growth - It Is Normal To Fear Change.

"Blessed is the one who has discovered that there is NOTHING permanent in life but change!"
A.P.Gouthey

I look forward to change.

Change is progress.

I handle change with anticipation
and positive expectation.

Progress is exciting - I look forward to
the challenges awaiting me.

I have faith in myself. I can handle
change and create opportunities
for personal growth and fulfillment.

Learning Increases My Self Confidence !

"Education is the ability to listen to almost anything without losing your temper or your self-confidence."
                                       Robert Frost

Every time I finish a good book, I am more understanding of humankind.

With every good conversation with friends, I have more confidence in my abilities to learn more.

A good education can be acquired in everyday circumstances. I am always open to learn from others.

"When books are opened, you discover you have wings."
                              Helen Hayes

I Love Challenges !

CHALLENGE: Anything that calls for special effort; a contest.

The chosen ones are challenged, the more they endure, the more they have to give back !

I greet challenges with enthusiasm.

I believe I am chosen to lead a happy, fulfilling, rewarding life.

Challenges are exciting and stimulating.

When challenged, I do my very best and I am proud of my efforts.

Power

*"My philosophy is that
not only are you responsible
for your life, but doing
the best at this moment
puts you in the best place
for the next moment."*

Oprah Winfrey

*"Great works are performed, not by
strength, but by perseverance."*

Samuel Johnson

Who Am I ?

"Wherever I go, there I am."
                                        Aristotle

Since I am with me everywhere,
 I shall be:
  My best friend,
  My greatest colleague,
  My mentor,
  My confidant.

I like and respect myself.

I know I am a worthy, capable and valuable person.

I counsel with myself to do what is best for me.

I am capable of expressing myself and I know others respect my point of view.

"Who I am makes a difference !"
Susan Jeffers

I Use The Power I Was Pre-Programmed With To Meet The Challenges Of Life.

My subconscious mind is constant energy and it never sleeps.

When I feel an intuition, I listen to it - my subconscious mind is guiding me.

I have everything to gain by listening to my subconscious.

I trust my subconscious.

When I have a goal that isn't working out, I surrender to my subconscious for re-programming.

My subconscious chooses what is best for me.

I follow my intuition.

I Am Magnificent !

I Take Charge Of My Life !

I have the power to take myself from where
I am now to where I choose to be !

I realize there can be no vacuums,
therefore, I substitute desirable
habits for undesirable habits !

The power of repetition is the "glue"
to make my desired changes "stick!"

I know it takes at least eleven (11)
insertions to change a habit.

I constantly remind myself . . .
I can be whoever
and whatever
I choose to be !

"Build therefore your own world.
As fast as you conform your life
to the pure idea in your mind,
that will unfold into great proportions."
                                   Ralph Waldo Emerson

In My Infinite Wisdom When I Choose To Make Changes In My Life And In My Personality, I KNOW I CAN !

I am endowed with the power to make the best decisions for me. When I surrender to that power, I have the courage to take the steps necessary to reach my goals.

When I don't reach my goal on the first "leap," I leap again !

"Don't be afraid to take a big step if one is indicated. You can't cross a chasm in two small jumps."
　　　　　　　　　　　David Lloyd George

I Can Handle Fear !

I handle my fear of the unknown
with the faith that I am meant to be
magnificent.

I AM IN CONTROL.

I CAN HANDLE FEAR.

I CAN HANDLE ANYTHING !

By doing what I fear, I conquer it !

I act with courage and take the initiative
in becoming a success at whatever
I choose to do, to have, to become.

**I always have courage . . .
I am courageous !**

I Become More Powerful Every Day !

"Knowledge is power, but imagination is more powerful."
　　　　　　　　　　Albert Einstein

I see the wonders that I can accomplish.

I accomplish something worthwhile everyday.

I see the people I can inspire.

I feel the power with which
God has graced me.

I love sharing what my imagination sees.

"Whatever the mind of man can conceive and believe, it can acheive."
　　　　　　　　　　Napoleon Hill

I Am Positive !
I Am Powerful !
I Am A Leader !

I am a positive influence on others by
my generosity of time, energy,
abilities and other resources.

I look for ways to unselfishly
build others up.

I am a competent leader and I encourage
others to reach their full potential.

I am my own expert - and I allow others
the same privilege.

I repay others who have helped me by
passing it on and expecting
the best from others.

*"Every heart that has beat strong and
cheerfully has left a hopeful impulse
behind it in the world, and bettered
the tradition of mankind."*
Robert Louis Stevenson

I Understand The Three Types Of Power:

1. **Knowledge:** I plan my studies and follow through. I am always learning. I love growing in knowledge - it keeps me ALIVE and WELL !

2. **Personal:** I am a valuable person. My self confidence is contagious. Others enjoy being around me. I am generous with my time and my ideas to help others.

3. **Position:** I am growing more confident in myself, in my position and in my career all the time.

**I am powerful and I love it . . .
and I share it !**

I Am A Leader !

I know what I want !

I know what I want to do !

I know what I'm doing !

I quickly learn what I need to know to advance my interests !

I am "on deck"
and
ready to sail.

I have the rudder down and the course mapped out.

I am confident in my choices.

My happiness makes others around me happy !

My inner power confirms my decisions.   I use the Universal Power to help me as a leader.

I Stay On My Chosen Path.

Today I CHOOSE to make decisions
that have been holding me back
from my heart's desire !

I know what I want and I do what
it takes to accomplish my goals.

I make choices that are good for ME.

I trust myself.

I follow through on my choices.

I always make choices carefully.

I trust in the Universal Power.

I trust in my own power.

I USE MY POWER !

If it can be done, I CAN do it !

Growth

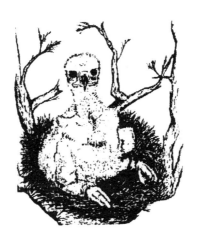

"Find a job you enjoy and are good at and you'll never work another day in your life."

Confuscious

"Come along grow with me, for the Best Is Yet To Be !"

Robert Browning

I Want A New Direction.

I have confidence in my decisions.

I guide my own destiny and I am
accountable for the results of
my decisions and actions.

I reinforce my successes and correct
the direction as needed.

I frequently visualize what I want
most from life.

I see myself succeeding and happy.

I trust my intuition - it guides me in
the best path for me. I am strong.

I consult my innermost feelings to
find my direction in life.

I have a purpose.

I Love Hearing And Acting On New Ideas !

"One's mind stretched to a new idea never goes back to its original dimensions."
Oliver Wendell Holmes

I enjoy trying new things.

Personal growth is exciting.

I continue to search for my aptitude.

I am comfortable in new situations.

My life is constantly enriched by reading and listening to tapes.

"Fortune sides with him who dares."
Virgil

I Can Grow To Become The Person I Want To Be.

I, Me, My, Mine, Myself are Wonderful Words.

I am a wonder-full person !

I talk to myself first person, "I", and teach myself what I want to know and need to know to live my life more abundantly.

I resolve to live today to the fullest, and when today is over, I rest well and anticipate a wonderful tomorrow.

I easily anticipate and experience events in my imagination before they actually happen.

I expect my life to be exciting and rewarding.

Every New Day Is A Challenge !

"Though no one can go back and make a brand new start, anyone can start from now and make a brand new end."
Debby Clinton

I accept the past as it is. I know I cannot change it.

I forgive myself and others for things in my past that I do not like.

I do not dwell on things I cannot change; I think of the good things.

I look forward each day to a new beginning.

Each day is a new opportunity to love, to care, to share, to achieve.

I look forward to the challenges of each new day.

I Am Healthy !
I Am Full Of Energy !

I exercise regularly and get plenty of rest.

I maintain my ideal weight.

I eat only foods that are good for me.

I enrich my mind with good thoughts as I enrich my body with good food.

Using affirmations controls the stress created by everyday challenges.

By taking care of myself, I am better able to give to those I love and to share with others I want to help.

"Compassion for myself is the most powerful healer of them all."
Theodore Issac Rubin

I Am Proud Of
Being Very Effective.

I have pride in my performance and a positive expectancy of the future.

I am patient with myself.

I am patient with others.

I avoid putting pressure on myself to hurry, or to accomplish too fast.

I know there is a time for everything and my subconscious leads me in setting and reaching goals.

I am proud of my follow through.

I always finish my projects.

"Be not afraid of going slowly, be afraid only of standing still."
                                    Chinese Proverb

My Energy Is Exciting !

I wake up enthusiastic every morning

When I have many responsibilities and feel overwhelmed, I remind myself:

My energy is boundless !

I love action !

I love activity !

I love responsibility !

I love life !

"Nothing in the world can take the place of persistence. Talent will not; nothing is more common than unsuccessful men with talent. Genius will not; unrewarded genius is almost a proverb. Education alone will not; the world is full of educated derelicts. Persistence and determination alone are omnipotent."
Calvin Coolidge

I Am Very Talented !

"Use the talents you possess; for the woods would be very silent if no birds sang except the very best."
                                    Author Unknown

I use my talent in very creative ways.

I learn something new everyday.

My talent is a gift for which I am thankful.

I use the talents I have to make my life better.

I share my talents in helping others.

I expect to become more talented in other areas - I am receptive to ideas offered to me by others.

"What people say you cannot do, you try and find that you can."
                                    Thoreau

I AM VERY CREATIVE !

I make the most ordinary happening
Extra-ordinary by seeing the
miracle in humanity !

I am willing to try new things and
overcome my fear of the unknown.

I am endowed with a questioning mind
and want to create to benefit others.

I create smiles, greetings, notes, and
ideas that delight the people I meet.

My day is always better when I can
share some of my creative fun.

My mind is awesome and always busy
with exciting ideas.

**The more I please others,
 share ideas, give away,
  the greater I feel !**

I AM AS A LITTLE CHILD !

*"Suffer little children to come unto
me for of such is the kingdom of God."*
Luke 19:16

I rejoice in everything around me.

I see wonder everywhere.

I love getting up in the morning to
see what the day will bring.

My life is good and full of wonder.

When people ask me "how are you?"
I answer "Fantastic !"

I spread my joy to others.

"Genius is childhood recaptured."
Charles Baudelaire

Friends

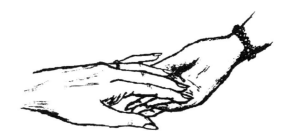

"I have learned that to have a good friend is the purest of all God's gifts, for it is a love that has no exchange of payment."

Frances Farmer

"We are all travelers in the wilderness of this world, and the best that we find in our travels is an honest friend."

Robert Louis Stevenson

Friendship Is A Gift
I Give Myself.

"Let there be no purpose in friendship save the deepening of the spirit."
        Kahlil Gibran

One true friend in a lifetime is a treasure.

I have found a true friend and I love and respect her for her honesty and compassion.

I am patient when my friend has a problem. I understand and care.

My friends help me to see things as they are or as they could be.

I trust my friends to share the truth with me.

I have many friends in whom
I take great joy.

I appreciate my friends.

"Friends are my windows on the world."
        Will Oursler

Everyone Needs Someone !

"A friend is a person with whom I may be sincere. Before my friend, I may think aloud."
                                Emerson

Everyone needs someone to listen.

I practice being a good listener. I do not offer advice - just listen and feel the pain or the pleasure with my friend.

I am trustworthy and never betray a confidence.

I will fight to defend my friendships.

I know that to have a friend, I must first be a friend.

I am my own best friend too !

"One who is his own friend, is a friend to all."
                                Seneca

I Enjoy Finding And Keeping Friends.

"Friends are my windows on the world."
Will Oursler

I have the courage to find new friends everywhere, every day.

I am thrilled by the uniqueness of the people I meet.

I am comfortable meeting new people.

I go "out of my way" to meet and get to know others.

I am always truthful with my friends.

I respect my friends.

I am a reflection of my friends.

"The happiest moments of my life have been in the flow of affection among friends."
Thomas Jefferson

Friends Are a Great Treasure !

*"The heart of one who speaks rests itself on
the heart of the friend who listens."*
Countess DuBerry

Today I will find new friends to enjoy and help.

I am a great listener - I enjoy encouraging
others to tell me of their dreams and goals.

I look for the good in people and
I expect the best.

My life is richer for each friend I find and
share myself with.

I surrender to the experiences I encounter.
I make them better when I can.

*"Treat people as if they were what they
ought to be and you help them become
what they are capable of being."*
Johann Wolfgang Van Goethe

Each Person I Meet Is One Of God's Valuable Children.

"Inasmuch as ye have done it unto one of the least of these my brethren, ye have done it unto Me."
Matthew 25:40

Each of us is fighting a hard battle in life -
the challenge of personal growth
and responsibility.

I understand this, and I am kind.

I pray for the strength to handle my own
battle and help others in theirs.

"Walk as children of light, for the fruit of the Spirit is in all goodness, and righteousness and truth."
Ephesians 5: 8, 9

I Am Outgoing And Initiate New Contacts.

"I'll make them glad they met me !"
Will Rogers

Today I will find new friends
to enjoy and help.

My life is richer for each friend I find
and share myself with.

I am a good listener and I care about what
others are saying.

When others are not as considerate as
I would like them to be,
I understand and forgive.

I have a service that is beneficial.

I always conduct myself as if
I am a good friend.

I keep in touch with friends and
associates alike.

I Am Comfortable Meeting New People !

*"It is the common wonder of all men,
how among so many millions of faces,
there should be none alike."*
                                    Sir Thomas Browne

I am thrilled by the uniqueness of the people I meet.

I go "out of my way" to meet and get to know others.

I am a great listener - I enjoy encouraging others to tell me of their dreams and goals.

*"Each friend represents a world in us,
a world possibly not born until
they arrive; and it is only by this meeting
that a new world is born."*
                                    Ana is Nin

I Look For The Good In People - I Expect The Best.

"Every experience God gives us, every person He puts in our lives, is the perfect preparation for the future that only He can see."

Corrie ten Boom

I surrender to the experiences I encounter.

I make them better when I can.

I eagerly anticipate meeting new people - new friends.

People are in my life and I in theirs for a purpose.

"Friendship hath the skill and observation of the best physician, the diligence and vigilance of the best nurse, and the tenderness and patience of the best mother"

Edward Clarendon

Love

*"To unite we must
love one another;
to love one another
we must know one another;
to know one another
we must meet one another."*

Desire Joseph Mercier

*"To love is to receive
a glimpse of heaven."*

Karen Sunde

I Am Happy !

*"Happiness comes not from having much
to live on, but having much to live for."*
                        Tyrone Edwards

When I feel lonely and alone,
I ponder all the good I can do.

Happiness cannot be "bought".

Money is good for the benefit
it can create in lives, but
my love for sharing
is my real happiness.

*"To be of use in the world is the
only way to be happy."*
                        Hans Christian Anderson

What Do I "Owe" Myself?

Love and hugs.
    Personal power.
        Privacy when I want it.
            Time to dream.
                Happy expectations.
                    Enthusiasm for life.
                        Belief in my success!

I am ageless - my mind becomes keener with each passing day!

I owe myself youthful thinking, feeling, and actions.

I owe myself happiness.

It's okay to be happy!

*"Whoever is happy will
make others happy too."*
Anne Frank

What Do I "Owe" Others ?

I owe my spouse a happy spouse,
love, and consideration !

I owe my children a happy parent
and unconditional Love !

Children learn what they see -
they need to SEE happiness.

I owe my employer a cooperative,
happy employee.

I owe my parents respect -
"honor thy father and mother."

I owe my friends loyalty,
respect, and attention.

**Eighty-five percent of my joy and
pleasure in life involves others !**

I Remind Myself -
The More I Share,
The More I Have !

The multitude were fed with only
five loaves of bread and two fish.

I love sharing what I have - what I know -
what I have learned from those
who have shared with me.

I share what the Universal Power
can do for us when we use it.

PEOPLE ARE SUGGESTIBLE !

I set the example by sharing and caring.
Others follow my example and pass it on !

I Have Great Joy In Living And Loving !

"There's a spring in my step,
a lilt in my walk . . .
There's life in my thoughts
and joy in my talk."
Carleen Franklin

I am very loving, and I am loved !

I learn from every ordinary,
everyday adventure I encounter.

I choose to make this day, this minute
memorable with my love of life.

**There is a radiance about me that enthuses
others and draws them to me.**

I Am Very Loving !

"The ultimate lesson all of us have to learn is unconditional love, which includes not only others but ourselves as well."
                                Elizabeth Kubler-Ross

I love and respect myself.

I know I am a worthy, loving, and lovable person.

My heart is open to those who need love and I am generous.

Love enriches the soul.

*"Kindness in words creates confidence.
Kindness in thinking creates profoundness.
Kindness in giving creates love."*
                                Lao-Tze

Faith

*"Faith is to believe
what we do not see,
and the reward of faith is
to see what we believe."*

St. Augustine

*"If you have faith as a grain
of mustard seed . . nothing
shall be impossible to you."*

Matthew 17:20

Out Of Suffering Comes The Strongest Souls. Gods Wounded Often Make The Best Soldiers.

"One's life has value so long as one attributes value to the life of others, by means of love, friendship, indignation and compassion."
                        Simone de Beauvoir

I understand those who have wronged or disappointed me and I forgive their actions.

We are all human, and subject to human frailties.

"Be not afraid of life. Believe that life is worth living, and your belief will help create the fact."
                        William James

What I Can Be
I Already Am !

"In every child who is born, under no matter what circumstances, and of no matter what parents, the potentiality of the human race is born again."
James Agee

GREAT power is preprogrammed within me !

I accept that I am powerful !

I have faith in my power !

I have faith in my mission in life !

Faith precedes the miracle !

I believe I am a miracle !

"How many cares one loses when one decides not to be something, but to be someone."
Coco Chanel

My Reactions To A Situation Determine Its Power To Affect My Life And Happiness.

It's not what happens to me - it's how I react to it that determines the results.

I always assume the best in a situation.

I am careful to consider advice.

I let others help me, and I help myself.

I consider all situations an opportunity even when I don't understand "why?"

All things work together for the good of those who believe . . .

I BELIEVE !

Every Person In My Life Is Significant !

I am important - I am significant !

I am exactly where I am supposed to be.

EVERY person I meet is important !

Every person is in my life for a purpose !

We each have a mission in life -
we teach what we need to learn.

I open my mind and my heart to my mission
and I know, I believe, I affirm,
I am meant to fulfill myself.

*"There are no insignificant people.
there is no one who isn't supposed
to be there."*
                                Hugh Prather

I Look Forward To Challenges - Life Would Be Very Dull Without Them.

*"What we are is God's gift to us.
What we become is our gift to God."*
　　　　　　　　　　Eleanor Powell

I pray for God to show me His plans for me.

I feel I have a mission in life according
to his plan.

I do what I "have to do" and
my subconscious is guiding me.

*"Our prayers are not answered when
we are given what we ask, but when we
are challenged to be what we can be."*
　　　　　　　　　　Morris Adler

When I Don't Succeed, I Surrender !

"Faith is the bird that feels the light and sings when the dawn is still dark."
            R.Tagore

When I am trying very hard and
things I think I want aren't coming together,
I *surrender* and turn the problem
over to my subconscious mind.

My subconscious is plugged into the power
of the universe and has the answers I seek.

FAITH preceeds the MIRACLE !

I have faith that my subconscious mind
will find the best path for me and
guide me to personal fulfillment.

We Are Never More Discontented With Others Than When We Are Discontented With Ourselves.

I understand there are times when
I must evaluate my feelings.

I deal with my own feelings gently.

I deal with the feelings of others gently.

By striving to understand my own feelings,
I am better able to understand others.

I am patient with myself.

I am patient with others.

*"If it be possible, as much as lieth
in you, live peaceably with all men."*
Romans 12:18

I Am Courageous !

**I have the courage to gaze at the
mountains and believe I can climb them.**

I never let the grain of sand
in my shoe stop my climb.

The view from the mountain top
is worth the climb.

From the top I can see the Eagles
flying so close
I can almost touch them !

I BELONG WITH THE EAGLES -

COURAGEOUS AND FREE !

I AM FREE - I AM ME !

I CAN FLY ! ! ! !

Affirmations

Affirmations Help Me Make Changes !

Affirmation: A one sentence definition of a quality, a characteristic, a habit, or a material goal one may desire. It may be tangible or intangible.

Using affirmations is a technique proven to help us to build new habits, set and reach goals, eliminate negatives and replace them with positive qualities. We are proud to share this technique !

It takes doing something only twice to make it a habit - it takes from eleven to twenty-two insertions to change a habit.

> **"If you want a quality, pretend you already have it."**
> Norman Vincent Peale

Affirmations are like Dr. Peale's quote. To make a change, reach a goal, or have a quality, I act as I would if it is already a fact.

To install affirmations in my mental computer is a three (3) step process:

STEP 1: COMPOSING THE AFFIRMATION

(1) Choose the change item

(2) Word it in first person -
    I, me, my, mine

(3) Word it present tense -
    is, now, have, do

(4) Must be realistic -
    "possible"

(5) Make it specific -
    as detailed as possible

(6) Use my emotions -
    happy, love, proud

STEP 2: INSTALLING AFFIRMATION

PRINT out on 3 x 5 or 5 x 8 cards.

Use one sentence per card.

Rewrite one affirmation several ways.

Read affirmations several times a day - optimum times morning and evening.

Place copies of them everywhere.

Some are private and confidential.

Tape record in my own voice and listen whenever possible.

Visualize - actually see in my mind my goal coming true.

I rewrite and reevaluate my affirmations as I achieve a goal.

STEP 3: USING AFFIRMATIONS

Incorporate feelings while reading or listening to the affirmations.

Use emotional words in affirmations and feel the emotions while reading them, for this has greater impact on the subconscious mind.

Examples:

I love the smell of my new blue car.

My new living room furniture looks beautiful with the new carpet.

I'm proud to be maintaining my ideal weight.

I love to exercise and I feel great.

I eat only foods that are good for me.

I get excited when I think of what I can do with my higher salary.

My savings account is a great comfort.

I love my new direction and I am very happy !

They that wait
 upon the Lord
Shall renew
 their strength.

They shall mount up with
 wings like Eagles.

They shall run
 and not be weary,
They shall walk
 and not faint.

Isaiah 40:31

About The Authors

Carleen's family moved to central Florida from upstate New York when she was three years old; their first job was picking and packing fruit. She lived in seventeen places before she was eleven years old, including the cab of an "18 wheeler" while her parents delivered fruit.

This chaotic childhood resulted in feelings of neglect and insecurity which she has been fighting all her life. Having a four year high school average of 97, she was offered two college scholarships. Not "seeing" herself in college she turned them both down.

Her journey from "pitiful" to "powerful" is the basis of this book. She now flies with the Eagles by helping others find their "wings".

Sarah comes from an average, middle class family in Tennessee, the second of four children of happy, church going parents. She grew up the quiet, shy one of the family and became a registered nurse because she says she had no real direction and knew she could always get a job. After moving to Vero Beach with her husband and son, Sarah became a member of Carleen's direct sales organization.

Sarah, recognized in the top twenty-five of 10,000 managers nationwide, credits her success to the personal empowerment and self management techniques that are shared in this book.

Carleen and Sarah, internationally known as the *Excelerators*, present seminars, workshops and sales training to help "Accelerate the Excellence Within."

NATIONAL
SPEAKERS
ASSOCIATION